THIS LAND CALLED AMERICA: **CALIFORNIA**

CREATIVE EDUCATION

Published by Creative Education
P.O. Box 227, Mankato, Minnesota 56002
Creative Education is an imprint of The Creative Company
www.thecreativecompany.us

Book and cover design by Blue Design (www.bluedes.com)
Art direction by Rita Marshall
Printed in the United States of America

Photographs by Getty Images (Archive Holdings Inc., Brian Bahr, Jusin
Bailie, ROBYN BECK/AFP, GABRIEL BOUYS/AFP, Jeff Foott, Hackett/
Archive Photos, Timothy Hearsum, William S. Helsel, Hulton Archive,
John Kobal Foundation, Kean Collection, James Martin, David Paul Morris,
Timothy H. O'Sullivan, Panoramic Images, James Randklev, Lorne Resnick,
Nicolas Russell, Zia Soleil, Inga Spence, Stock Montage/Stock Montage,
Ron & Patty Thomas, Carleton Emmons Watkins, Tim Zurowski)

Library of Congress Cataloging-in-Publication Data
Peterson, Sheryl.
California / by Sheryl Peterson.
p. cm. — (This land called America)
Includes bibliographical references and index.
ISBN 978-1-58341-630-3
1. California—Juvenile literature. I. Title. II. Series.
F861.3.P48 2008
977.4—dc22   2007005683

First Edition
9 8 7 6 5 4 3 2 1

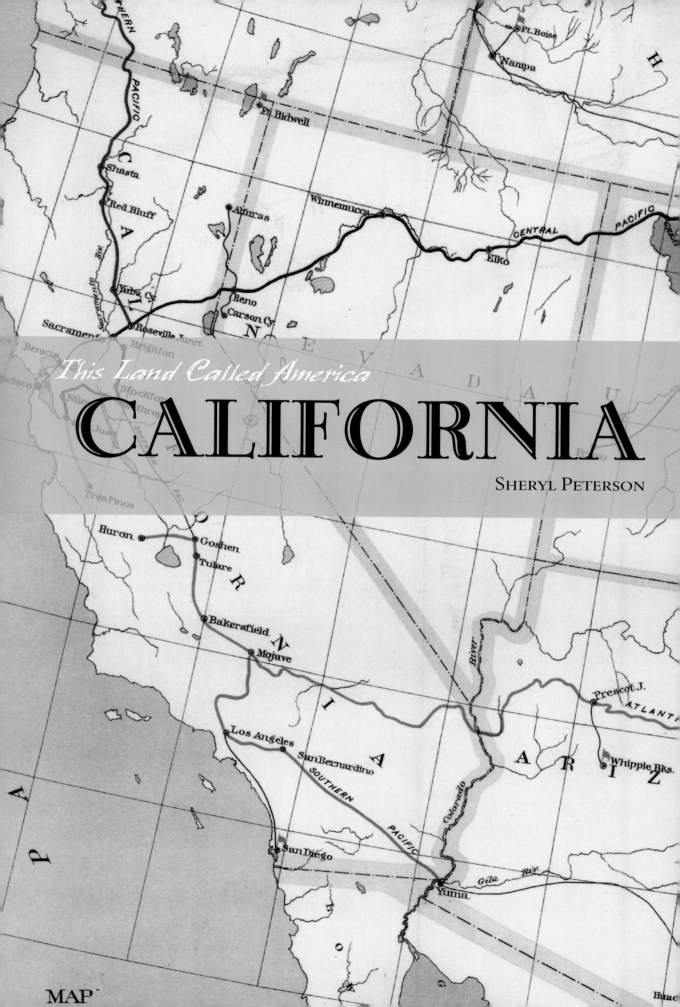

This Land Called America

CALIFORNIA

SHERYL PETERSON

This Land Called America

California

SHERYL PETERSON

White sand sifts between bare toes. Turquoise waves swish in at the shore. Sea gulls swoop down over a California beach. Out in the Pacific Ocean, surfers and boogie-boarders paddle out to catch the next big wave. Kids carry plastic buckets and shovels and use them to build giant sandcastles. Beneath the palm trees, local artists display their crafts. A beach volleyball game begins as dune buggies speed by. When evening comes, people pile up dry wood and light bonfires on the sand. Everyone watches the sun sink below the Golden State's horizon. It's been another perfect California day at the beach.

YEAR
1769   Father Junipero Serra builds the first California mission.
EVENT

California, Here We Come!

Long before California was a state, the land held many American Indian villages. The Yuma, Hupa, and Paiute all had their own customs and languages. In 1542, Spanish explorers found California. Soon after, English people came. Neither of these groups built settlements in the region then. In the 1700's, Spanish Explorers took over Mexico and then headed north.

Father Junipero Serra and other Spanish Catholic priests began building outposts, or missions, in 1769. These settlements dotted the coastline along a rough road called El Camino Real, or "The King's Highway," which ran from San Diego in the south to San Francisco in the north.

In 1821, Mexico rebelled against Spain and became an independent country. The new Mexican leaders took charge in California as well. In 1836, explorer Jedediah Smith became the first American to travel across the country to California. As he crossed the deserts of Nevada and California, Smith sometimes had to bury himself in the sand to keep cool.

Miners (above) traveled across the country during the Gold Rush years and founded camps and makeshift towns such as Gold Hill (opposite).

YEAR

1826 The country of Mexico controls California after winning its independence from Spain.

EVENT

The California settlers who followed in Smith's footsteps wanted to be part of the United States. In 1844, U.S. Army officer John Fremont led a revolt against Mexico. His troops carried flags with pictures of bears on them, causing the movement to be known as the Bear Flag Revolt. (California's state flag today has an image of a bear on it to honor those brave men.) Soon, there was war between Mexico and the U.S. Both countries wanted California, but the U.S. won in 1848.

Once gold was discovered northeast of San Francisco in January 1848, the U.S. had more reasons to fight for California.

Gold nuggets were found in a stream near Sutter's Mill. John Sutter, the sawmill's Swiss owner, had tried to keep the discovery quiet, but soon the famous California Gold Rush began. In 1849, more than 80,000 prospectors, or gold miners, came to California. Some traveled by covered wagon across America. Others sailed up from South America. These newcomers were called "forty-niners."

Captain John Fremont (opposite) explored the West Coast and protected the rights of U.S. settlers who lived in the California foothills (above).

YEAR
1841   The first wagon train of settlers arrives in California.
EVENT

- 9 -

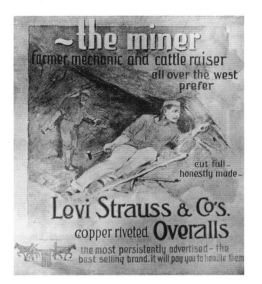

*In 1850, Levi Strauss
moved from Germany
to San Francisco, where
he made his first pair of
overalls.*

San Francisco, 1868

The miners needed supplies and places to sleep. Towns sprang up almost overnight to accommodate them. The new towns had names such as Rawhide, Humbug, and Rich Gulch. The city of San Francisco also grew rapidly. Huge ships carrying goods and miners cruised into its harbor.

Although few miners actually got rich, traveling salesman Levi Strauss made a fortune. He sold heavy pants made out of a canvas material. The durable pants became popular with the miners. They were the start of what people today know as Levi's jeans.

In 1850, California became the 31st state in the union. Over the next 10 years, Pony Express riders brought mail to California, and telegraph lines reached the state. People in the West could now get messages from the East quickly. The gold mines began to run dry, but people stayed in California. By 1860, there were 380,000 Californians.

Getting people and supplies to California was difficult until workers constructed a great railroad across America. Because it spanned the continent of North America, it was called the first transcontinental railroad. It was completed on May 10, 1869. Now people could easily travel from coast to coast.

YEAR

1849 The discovery of gold at Sutter's Mill starts the Gold Rush.

EVENT

Between 1835 and 1868, San Francisco grew from a one-tent dwelling into a booming port city.

The Golden State

CALIFORNIA IS THE THIRD-LARGEST STATE IN THE NATION. ONLY TEXAS AND ALASKA ARE BIGGER. IT IS BORDERED BY WASHINGTON TO THE NORTH. NEVADA AND ARIZONA FORM THE EASTERN BORDER. TO THE SOUTH IS BAJA CALIFORNIA, MEXICO.

California is a long state with many different landforms. The northern coast of California has steep, rocky cliffs. Below the cliffs is the pounding Pacific surf. Farther inland are mountains and forests. Redwood National Park is in northwestern California and is home to ancient redwood trees. Redwoods are the tallest trees in the world. The tallest tree in the park reaches 368 feet (112 m) into the air.

As redwood trees age, their lower branches fall away, leaving tall, smooth trunks.

The Sierra Nevada mountain range is the highest range in the continental U.S. California's Mount Whitney, at 14,505 feet (4,421 m), is the range's highest peak. Mount Whitney is part of Sequoia National Park, which has giant sequoia trees, too. Some are more than 200 years old. Yosemite National Park is also in the Sierra Nevadas. This park showcases magnificent waterfalls and steep canyons.

California's landscape features many hills covered with the state's official flower, the golden poppy.

Highway 1 runs along the Pacific Ocean's coast between Leggett in the north and San Juan Capistrano in the south. Many people think it offers some of the best scenery in the nation. The rugged cliffs, pounding surf, and rock formations carved out by the ocean's waves make for a thrilling drive. Along the way, people can stop in such historic cities as Monterey and Carmel-by-the-Sea.

YEAR

1869 California is linked with the East Coast by the transcontinental railroad.

EVENT

Central California grows most of America's fruits and vegetables. The region is cradled between the Coast Mountains and the Sierras. Farmers grow tomatoes, lettuce, and melons in the Central Valley. Nearby, ranchers raise beef cattle, sheep, and chickens.

Southern California, the area from Santa Barbara to the Mexican border, is dry and hilly. The weather is almost always warm. There are more than 100 miles (161 km) of white sand along the southern coast. Growers there tend groves of oranges and lemons.

Raising cattle (above) and growing crops (opposite) are important jobs in central California, whose Central Valley is America's largest agricultural area.

YEAR

1906   The San Francisco earthquake creates a massive fire that destroys hundreds of city blocks.

The Joshua tree is one of the few plants hardy enough to survive in California's Mojave Desert.

The Mojave Desert lies in southwestern California. It is one of the hottest places in the world. Death Valley is near the Nevada border. Temperatures there can get up to 130 °F (54 °C). Only strong plants such as barrel and beavertail cacti can survive in the sandy desert soil. Nearby, visitors may find monkey flowers and grizzly bear prickly pear trees.

All of California is not dry, though. California's two largest rivers are the San Joaquin and the Sacramento. They both flow through the Central Valley. The Colorado River is part of the state's border with Arizona. California shares its largest lake, the freshwater Lake Tahoe, with Nevada. Lake Tahoe is the 11th-deepest lake in the world.

YEAR
1937 — President Franklin Roosevelt gives the signal to officially open San Francisco's Golden Gate Bridge.
EVENT

Lake Tahoe, named for an Indian word meaning "big water," is 1,645 feet (501 m) at its deepest point.

The 1906 San Francisco earthquake caused damage to houses, sparked fires, and killed thousands.

Many wild animals live in California. Elk, bears, and deer roam the forests. Seals and sea otters swim in the waters off the Pacific coast. California condors, the largest birds in North America, are endangered. But they can still be seen once in a while.

Stretching from California's northern coast all the way to Mexico is the San Andreas fault line. Under this line are huge plates of rock that sometimes move, causing earthquakes. In 1906, a deadly earthquake struck San Francisco. In 1994, another quake shook the ground in Los Angeles. Highways collapsed, and many homes and properties were destroyed.

Despite the dangers of earthquakes, California's beaches and coastal views continue to attract people.

Sunny Californians

In the 1800s, thousands of settlers moved to California. Some looked for gold. Others were drawn to the warm climate. Starting in the early 1900s, people traveled to Hollywood to be stars in the movies.

Future president Ronald Reagan, shown here in 1939, soon after he left his job as a sportscaster to begin acting.

Today, people continue to come to California from all over the world. Although about half of the people in the state are white, many Californians do not speak English at home. More than 20 percent speak Spanish. Most of them live in the southern part of the state.

More Asian people live in California than in any other state. Chinese workers came to build the transcontinental railroad in the 1860s. Soon, people from countries such as Japan and Korea followed. African Americans make up about seven percent of California's population. The state has about 250,000 Native American residents, too. Only Oklahoma has more.

California has produced many famous people. Ronald Reagan was once an actor in Hollywood movies. He went on to become the 40th U.S. president in 1981. Richard Nixon was born in Yorba Linda and served as the 37th president. Tom Hanks is not a politician, but he is a popular California actor. The Concord native has starred in such movies as *Forrest Gump* and *The Polar Express*.

Many top athletes have come from California's sunny cities. Golfer Tiger Woods was born in Long Beach. In 1997, Woods became the first African-Asian American to win the Masters Golf Tournament. He was also its youngest winner at the age of 21. Woods's success prompted a surge of

Bixby Bridge, Big Sur

YEAR

1948 The largest telescope in the U.S. is constructed at California's Mount Palomar.

EVENT

California's scenic Big Sur region extends for about 100 miles (160 km) along the rocky Pacific coast.

YEAR

1955 Disneyland opens and attracts more than 50 million visitors over the next 10 years.

EVENT

- 21 -

interest in the game of golf among minorities and young people.

Florence Griffith Joyner was another superstar from California. Joyner was born in 1959 in Los Angeles and started running at age seven. She captured three gold medals at the 1988 Olympics in Seoul, Korea, and set records in the 100- and 200-meter dashes. Joyner was known for her long, colorful fingernails.

Michele Kwan is a famous figure skater from the Golden State. Kwan was born in Torrence, California. Her parents immigrated to the U.S. from Hong Kong. Kwan began skating at age five. She went on to win five world championships and nine U.S. figure skating titles.

Two well-known writers came from California. Jack London was born in San Francisco in 1876. He wrote *White Fang* and *Call of the Wild*. John Steinbeck, who wrote *The Grapes of Wrath*, came from Salinas. His book was made into a classic Hollywood film that starred Henry Fonda.

Jack London (opposite) and John Steinbeck (above) were two famous California authors of the early 1900s.

YEAR
1976   The Apple I personal computer is developed by Californians Steve Wozniak and Steve Jobs.
EVENT

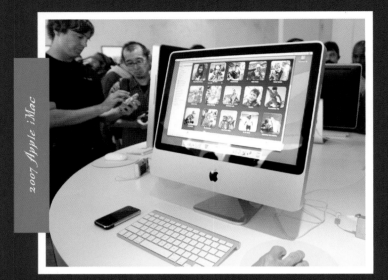

2007 Apple iMac

People have many different jobs in California. Some work in the aircraft industry. Engineers design and construct jet engines and spacecraft. Many people who live near San Francisco's Silicon Valley build computers and computer parts. Nearby, people grow grapes in the Napa Valley wine industry. Workers at the famous San Diego Zoo feed and care for many kinds of animals. Trainers at Sea World teach dolphins and seals to do tricks for visitors.

People still come to California to try to get rich or become famous. Others just come to relax in the sun. Most Californians can't imagine living anywhere else. They love the warm weather and the opportunities the state has to offer.

Silicon Valley is home to Apple, the maker of the iMac (above), and other electronics companies, while Hollywood (opposite) remains the home of American moviemaking.

YEAR
1981   Former California governor Ronald Reagan becomes U.S. president.
EVENT

Movie-Star State

CALIFORNIA IS A FAVORITE VACATION SPOT FOR FAMILIES.
EVERY YEAR, ABOUT 10 MILLION PEOPLE VISIT DISNEYLAND.
THIS MAGICAL AMUSEMENT PARK, LOCATED IN ANAHEIM,
SOUTH OF LOS ANGELES, OPENED ON JULY 18, 1955.
DISNEYLAND HAS BEEN CALLED "THE HAPPIEST PLACE ON
EARTH." KIDS CAN ZIP THROUGH THE DARK ON THE
SCARY SPACE MOUNTAIN RIDE OR SPIN CRAZILY IN A MAD

Chinese immigrants to San Francisco were forced to live in a separate part of the city, creating Chinatown.

Hatter's teacup. Visitors can stroll past Sleeping Beauty's Castle. They can shake hands with Mickey Mouse and Donald Duck.

San Francisco is another exciting place to visit. The city is in northern California along San Francisco Bay and the Pacific Ocean. Fisherman's Wharf is a popular tourist attraction by the bay. The piers are dotted with colorful seafood restaurants and shops.

Mickey Mouse, who has appeared in cartoons since 1928, is a popular attraction at Disneyland.

San Francisco is a very steep city. It is often called "the city of hills." Horses used to have a hard time pulling carriages up the hills. So Andrew Hallidie invented cable cars in 1873. Their bells still clang up and down the San Francisco hills today. Another special part of the city is Chinatown, which houses one of the nation's largest Asian communities.

YEAR

1995 The San Francisco 49ers football team wins its fifth Super Bowl.

EVENT

Visitors to Yosemite National Park enjoy rafting down the Merced River, which offers exciting rapids.

San Francisco's Golden Gate Bridge was finished in 1937 and is the city's most famous landmark.

In California's early days of statehood, some people came to the sunny state to make films. In 1911, the Nestor Company opened Hollywood's first film studio. Since then, thousands of movies have been shot there.

Visitors to Hollywood can tour Universal Studios and see how movies are made. Tourists can go behind the scenes in movies such as *Revenge of the Mummy* and *Back to the Future*. People can watch *Shrek* in 4-D. Nearby is the Hollywood Walk of Fame. Movie stars and other entertainers get a bronze star embedded in the special sidewalk to celebrate their achievements.

Californians also love their sports. On New Year's Day, the Rose Bowl is held in Pasadena, California. The Rose Bowl is a game between two football teams that are college conference champions. The Tournament of Roses Parade features floats that are decorated with fresh flowers.

California's large population makes it home to many professional sports teams—far more than any other state. The Los Angeles Dodgers and the San Francisco Giants are two of the state's five Major League Baseball teams. The Oakland

YEAR
2003
EVENT
Actor Arnold Schwarzenegger is elected governor of California.

- 28 -

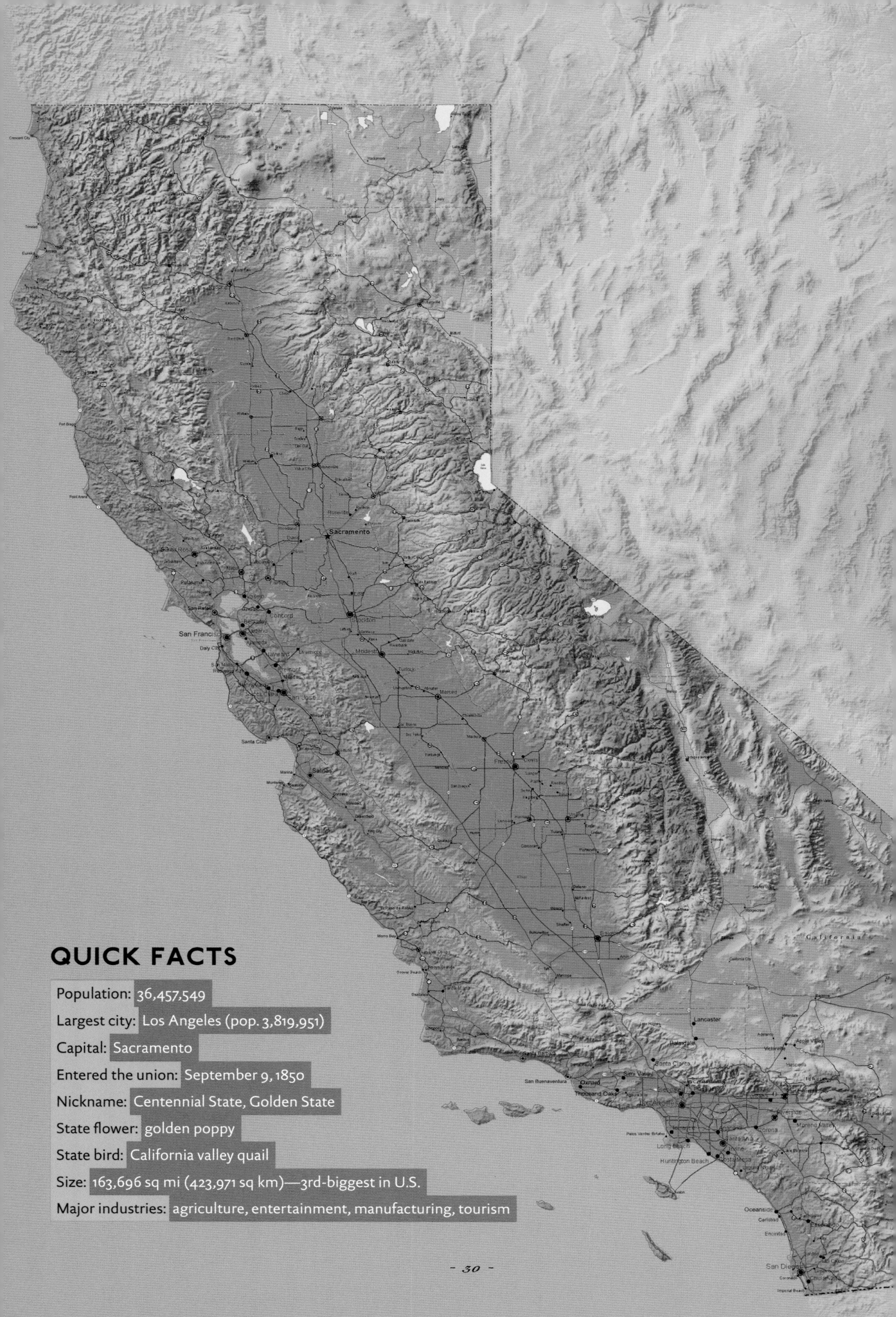

QUICK FACTS

Population: 36,457,549

Largest city: Los Angeles (pop. 3,819,951)

Capital: Sacramento

Entered the union: September 9, 1850

Nickname: Centennial State, Golden State

State flower: golden poppy

State bird: California valley quail

Size: 163,696 sq mi (423,971 sq km)—3rd-biggest in U.S.

Major industries: agriculture, entertainment, manufacturing, tourism

The San Francisco 49ers joined the National Football League in 1950 and have featured many famous players.

Raiders and San Francisco 49ers play in the National Football League. California also has top-level teams in basketball, hockey, and soccer.

Because of California's mild climate, people there are active. Residents rollerblade, bike, and swim almost year-round. California is known as the "surfing U.S.A." capital. Surfers can "catch a wave" or "ride the curl" in California's warm waters. For those who like non-aquatic activities, there is ample snow in the state's mountains for downhill skiing and cliffs for rock climbing.

The discovery of gold a century and a half ago transformed California's sleepy little villages into bustling cities. The state keeps growing today. If California were its own country, it would be the seventh-richest in the world. People sometimes worry that it will become one big, dirty supercity. They work hard to keep California's air and water clean.

The Golden State of California, full of many unique people and different types of jobs, is a great place to live. The state is blessed with natural beauty and a warm climate. People continue to travel west to California, the sunny land with endless possibilities.

BIBLIOGRAPHY

California State Railroad Museum. "Rails to the Pacific." California State Railroad Museum Foundation. http://www.csrmf.org/doc.asp?id=345.

Capstone Press Geography Department. *California*. Mankato, Minn.: Capstone Press, 1996.

Library of Congress. "Early California History: An Overview." California History Collection. http://www.csrmf.org/doc.asp?id=345.

Rowell, Galen. *California the Beautiful*. New York: Welcome Books, 2002.

Starr, Kevin. *Americans and the California Dream, 1850–1915*. Oxford: Oxford University Press, 1986.

———. *California: A History*. New York: Modern Library, 2007.

INDEX

American Indians 6, 20

animals 14, 18, 24

Bear Flag Revolt 8

border states 12, 16

Disneyland 26–27

earthquakes 18

first transcontinental railroad 10, 20

gold rush 9–10, 19, 31

   Sutter's Mill 9

Hanks, Tom 20

Highway 1 13

Hollywood 19, 20, 23, 28

industries 10, 14, 19, 20, 24, 28

   entertainment 19, 20, 28

   farming 14

   manufacturing 24

   ranching 14

   technology 24

Joyner, Florence Griffith 23

Kwan, Michelle 23

land regions and features 13–14, 16, 18, 31

   deserts 16

   forests 13, 18

lakes and rivers 16

   mountains 13, 14, 31

London, Jack 23

Los Angeles 18, 23, 26, 28

national parks 13

Nixon, Richard 20

Pacific Ocean 5, 13, 18, 27

plants 5, 13, 16

population 10, 19–20, 27

   countries represented 20

Reagan, Ronald 20

recreational activities 5, 31

San Francisco 9, 10, 18, 23, 27, 28, 31

Smith, Jedediah 7–8

Spanish explorers 6–7

sports 20, 23, 28

   professional teams 28, 31

state nickname 5, 23, 31

statehood 10

Steinbeck, John 23

Strauss, Levi 10

weather and climate 14, 16, 19, 24, 31

Woods, Tiger 20